<u>Octopus Magic</u>

By: Ellis James

❦Dedication❦

This book is dedicated to my wife, who has seen me in all of the ways I have not even seen myself. I love you to the moon and back. ♡

✳ Preface ✳

I lived most of my life as a cis-gendered woman. I spent my early years tugging at itchy dresses, and removing bows from my long hair. Pretty standard style for an 80's girl, but it for sure never felt good for me- never felt right.

For the record, I know that clothes do not have a gender. But I personally <u>do</u> feel more femme in a dress.

Thinking back, I remember finding joy in *pretending* that I was someone else. I recall using my leave-in conditioner to slick my hair back. Smiling as I would spray it and modify my appearance, *pretending* that I had short hair. Lathering up my face with potions I made in the bathroom, I would *pretend* that my beard needed shaving.

This continued for years, but in small amounts. Little sprinkles of joy in how I presented myself, thankfully leading to a huge ice cream sundae of gender euphoria later in my life.

My evolution as a Queer, Trans/Non-binary person, has NOT been an easy one. But with the right tools, support, and therapy I am growing and thriving.

Thank you for joining me along my journey, and thank you for letting me open my heart to you.♥

Table of Contents

◊Blades◊

The buzzer hit all of the tiny blades of hair. ◁
It exposed my soul and entire being
Raw and real
SCARY and enticing
Who is this person?
I didn't even recognize myself
But for the first time

I was not SHE. I was me. ☻

Around

Our **lips** met halfway
We both *leaned* in
They touched
It was enticing
It was electric
It was INCREDIBLE
It was a feeling I had yet to feel
In my 21 years on this earth
It was scary
I felt shame
I felt joy
I felt EXCITEMENT
I felt like I was soaring
I felt like I was unable to breathe
I drove home after with my windows open
Just to keep me in check ✔
I was high on life, and what my life looked like now
I was not this confused human
I was not this scared being

I was QUEER

Who are we ?

When did you first know who you were?
Was it the second you took that first breath?
Did your first kiss make you feel the most alive?
Or did it scare you in a way
That you could no longer relate to?
Why does it feel like coming out again?
I stopped recognizing my own body
Things started to feel different
I no longer recognized myself
When I looked in the mirror
Who am I? Who was I? Who am I supposed to be?

I am ME.

Taste

It feels like a century
It feels like that New Year's Eve kiss
That you waited all night for
You feel changed
You feel evolved
You realize you can never go back
Nothing will ever feel this good
The high
The rollercoaster
That terrifying feeling deep inside your stomach
The moment is on repeat in that gorgeous brain of
yours
We taste with your tongues

Your

Feelings

●

Warmth

When the tears flow ✛
They head down my cheek
They burn
They hurt
They process
Each tear stands for a different memory
Deep ones
Funny ones
Painful ones
When it lands, it glides down
Sometimes onto my paper
Smudging my writing
Making me start over
What is starting over?
Can we all just start over?
Imagine a world of do-overs.
Like if you messed up, you would get to start again.
Each bad experience could be corrected
When those tears flow. ✻

> *"Making*
> *Me*
> *Start*
> *Over".*

→Path

There is a path of life
There is a path of promise
There is a place we can be us
We can exist in a world in which we no longer feel
scared
We can exist in a world
In which our happiness trumps approval
And we can exist in a world
Where our bodies and our minds match
Path, there is a path of life. ←

"Body Matches Mind".

Cycles ⚧⚢

A stabbing pain shoots through your body
You grasp onto your stomach
The warm tears fall
The droplets hit the floor
You don't want this anymore
You are fearful
You are curious
You are unsure
You are excited
The stabbing pain hits harder
You begin to fall to the ground
You crawl into a fetal position
You no longer recognize yourself
This feeling every time..
A stabbing pain shoots through your body

*Leaf *

The leaf jumps
Onto the ground
Into a wet puddle
It gets stomped on
Crushed
Hurt
Broken
Tired
It blows into the wind
It keeps going
Despite getting stomped, and crushed, and hurt
It keeps going after being crushed
It keeps going after a piece of it has broken off
It keeps going long after it jumps

You
WERE
BrOkEN…

Poison

Be curious they said
Bite the fruit and be poisoned
Hide and be found
Love and be IN love
Hate only when you're hurt
Did that taste sweet?
Was it worth the pain?
Once the sugar glazed your lips
You tasted it
You loved it
You craved more
You were curious
You were poisoned

> "Once the sugar glazed your lips".

Band Aid

The bleeding heart drips
The blood flows down ↓
Where the Band Aid covers the wound
It does not allow for processing
And GRIEF
And pain
Rip that Band Aid slowly
Open up
Feel the pain
As the bleeding heart drips

Button

Loop the button through
Close the shirt
Those breaths no longer hurt
Wipe those feelings away
Up, up, and up you go
Feeling so high, like you could never let go
You feel it in your stomach
You feel it within your heart
It pumps hard like the blood
Going through your veins
You begin to shake
As you tremble in dismay
Let yourself feel
Ignore the hurt from before
Life is a rollercoaster
We keep coming back for more

The Red Dress

The color was the same as a fresh wound
It was bright, and had lace, and was itchy
It was the only one of its kind, but also was like
Everything I was forced to wear
It stuck to my body like a trap
It was impossible to get on and off myself
It made me feel like I was foreign
To my own body and appearance
It made me feel shame
All I wanted was a scissor to slice it to shreds
Cut through each piece of fabric and layer
Cut through each painful memory
Peel it away
Take it off, so that I can finally breathe
Heal the trauma

Alive

There is that feeling of being really tiny
Within a giant world
A small morsel of the **tiniest** crumb
A kiss that sends chills up your spine
A question of your entire body and being
What have you learned from feeling so alive?
Has it been worth the good?
In exchange for all of the pain?
The pain flows through your body within your blood
The blood travels to the surface, and you are awoken
From a dream, from traveling, from a bad experience
You stand up tall
You dust yourself off
You start fresh
You are no longer dreaming ☾
You are alive.

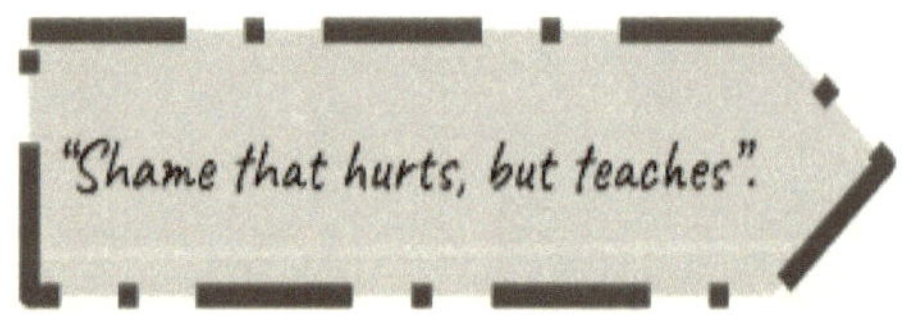

Electric

The force was transparent
It shot through like a beautiful orange spark
An orange so bright, it was like taking a bite of fruit
On that first spring day
A taste so sweet, you could still feel it
On your lips hours later, that day
There was a numbness
It acted like a reminder you were living
A touch that would make you burrow within your own skin
Feel every nerve pulsate as you got closer
It felt so heavy to breathe, but you were still breathing
It was electric

COLD

Have you ever felt cold and hot?
So cold that you are without a thought
So WARM that the fire inside you keeps you alive?
Fills every inch of your body and soul.
Brings the blood to your heart
As it beats faster and faster
Have you ever felt so thrilled that you felt invincible?
Life is about the hot and cold.
The strong, and the weak.
The love and the unloved.

♪)) ♪

Tighten

The first time I wore a tie
It felt so intense, I felt high
Like a bird flying
I had no fear of dying
It was a little tight
But it was worth the fight
Little childhood me
Felt bliss within a symphony
The **MUSIC** played loud
Amongst a large crowd
The tears pouring
My heart soaring
I reached for my neck
And I smiled with glee
It felt warm, like that
First sip of tea
The first time I wore that tie

Teardrops

The tears drip...
The heart pounds...
The pain rips you apart, yet holds you together
The planets are moving
The feeling is hurting
Move forward and stop the hurt they say
Just walk away-okay?

Monsters In *The* |Closet|

The cold breeze from an open window
It sneaks in
It tickles your nose
It sends you into a whirlwind of fear
It tornados you down
It messes up your hair
It changes your vibe
It makes you feel worthless
It feels dark
Like you have never felt the warmth
Of the bright yellow sun
Opening the door feels impossible
You pull, and you push, and you lean

LEANING feels unfeasible
You feel like a burden
You feel like a Monster
You're the Monster in the closet

Fog

When breathing deep <u>HURTS</u>
You feel like you can't cry anymore
And rock bottom feels like a galaxy
That you have passed over and over again
Those tears fall so hard and fast
You are drowning in your own pain
You're scared..
Deep inside you know it
We are all scared
Life is sacred
Filled with moments
That make our heart beat a little harder
Moments that make us feel like we are floating
People that make us breathe a little deeper
And one day–
Those breaths no longer ache
They still feel cold
They still feel scary
They fog up our windows
They keep us warm
They hold us tight
They support us
Take that breath
Just breathe...

Feel

Let yourself feel
But not too much
When the pressure builds up
And it may be too late
You instantly begin
To reflect on that hate
You want to feel happiness
Like that beautiful first date
Remember how that kiss felt?
Or how cold the air felt
When her lips left yours?
How you knew she was your forever
Just because
Your souls were intertwined
From that very first day
For good and for bad
Like the sun shining in May

Imperfection

The timing will vary for all
It depends massively on
When you get that call
Suddenly it's not rainbows that make you fall
It's the dark clouds that inspire you
The wrinkles, the kindness, that make you feel smitten
It is not the life, that you once saw written
The timing will vary for all

Fire And Foundation

Contain it
Let it go
Build it up
Spray it and frown
Climb the ladder
Get knocked down

The Addition

I took away my long hair
And there it was short
I changed my name
Because the last one
It *hurt*
I took several trips around the sun
Until one trip, really felt like
The one
A euphoric example
Of how it is done
What is this feeling I felt?
A feeling of pain, that I had only dwelt
I had my masc days, and my femme days
And all that was in between
I lost people, and gained people
In a world that felt so unclean
We are all masters within our universe
It is ok to cry in this world, it is ok to rewrite your
verse.

E U P H O R I C

Delicious *Mistakes*

It was just like that frigid ice pop
It dripped down onto your brand new white shoes
You know those shoes
The ones your Mom told you
Not to ruin
But you did
They were no longer white
They were rainbow

You gasped in fear
And as you inhale deeply
You are instantly reminded
That what was cold and scary
Was also a delicious mistake

BoneS

When you feel different
You feel it deep down
Beneath your skin
Beneath your bones
Deeper than one would ever really know
But it's there
It's so fresh
It feels like such a mess
You can't change it
You can't reshape

Rollercoaster

Buckle up, and face your fears
Live a life of dreams
Wipe those feelings away
Up, up, and up you go
Feeling so high, like you could never let go
You feel it in your stomach
You feel it within your heart
It pumps hard like the blood
Going through your veins
You begin to shake
As you tremble in dismay
Let yourself feel
Ignore the hurt from before
Life is a Rollercoaster
We keep coming back for more

Darkness Within

The clock is ticking
The time is up
Move forward you must
Or get left back
Dust yourself off as they say
Can you just move on
Without being right
Each day?
Have the last word
The final sip of tea
Ouch you've been burned
And it is not the first time
The darkness within haunts you
For your entire life
Ringing in your ears
The noise in your brain
Shut off the sound
You just can't hear it again
It stings
It hurts
It burns like fire
The pain is unlike any ordinary cut
It will be there forever

Gender

Have you ever felt whole?
Embodied as one?
Or have you felt confused?
Like your entire body
Never felt ONE
From a very young age
You were placed in a box
And at the same time
You were constantly mocked
Don't do this
Don't do that
You were told
From a very YOUNG age
You rarely saw yourself
Growing old
But one day this all changed
And you finally felt comfortable within your skin
It was a very memorable day
You finally felt right within

Sick

It started deep down
The pain was so intense
It caused you to frown
You know it did not make sense
It was hard to pinpoint
What was causing this pain

It stemmed from *childhood*
Where nothing felt the same
The others were nothing like you
You rarely fit in
There was the time you felt at home
You placed your hat backwards
You were FINALLY able to take that
Deep breath in
It stopped you in your tracks
It hurt your ribs
It felt like a cold December day
It was in that moment
You felt sick

Roll Of The Dice

A roll of the dice
It should give you an answer
For which side do you prefer?
How will you tell?
Are you happy when you pass?
Unhappy when you fail?
Euphoric when someone has to guess?
Confused at it all?
A goodbye
Like the last time you spoke
It was a distant memory
For you were not
Who you are now
You made more enemies
Not by your own choosing
But from your own learning
You leveled up each year
You grew more understanding
That last goodbye
Felt similar as the first hello
It left the same impression on your lips
It imprinted the same mark on your soul

The Clouds

Puffy cotton clouds consume my thoughts
Take over them entirely
I watch them move
Across the world
They shape and shift
Like I wish I could do
So I can feel at home
So I can look like you want me to

The Blinding Sun

Shut the window
Draw the curtains
Stop the frigid air that
Blows through each strain of hair
The dizzy spells control you
Spins you around
Lifts you right up
Knocks you right down
Makes you reconsider
Time is running out
You can't help but pout
The feeling goes deep
In the pit of your stomach
You stop letting them in
Like the blinding sun

"Don't Let The Dizzy Spells CONTROL You"

Purple

It was the hue of the two colors mixed
It had a shiny glaze
My entire life is a maze
It made me question
It gave me answers
It was a bruise on my knee
That stayed for ages
It was all part of the growing process
It was charming like the storm ridden sky
It was purple.

✳ Alluring ✳

The way they looked
And the way they looked at you
The snap of their fingers
The effect they had on you
The smell was so intoxicating
It drew you in further
It made you disorientated
Like a ride at the carnival
You were unsure if they would catch you
But when you began to fall,
They helped you rise up

Insecure

Each one felt right
Like you could not wear it
With all of your might
They punched
They left marks
Little cuts on the sides ↔
Little traces in the front
They pressed them closer to your heart
You never felt more intolerable
You never felt more insecure

The 8 Ball 

Your turn
Your shot
Focus lightly
The 8 ball is hot
Pull back carefully
I wish you luck
For I was no longer the same
Since I changed that night
For I had evolved
Like a caterpillar
Beautiful
And flying away
To escape the fiery 8 ball

Bound

To feel restrained
To feel whole
To feel trapped
To feel like you would never reach your goal
To worry about others
And never yourself
You were tired of the sound
The voice in your head
You were bound

O puntia

Like a cactus it pricks
Deep *Inside* it sits
Marking you from top to bottom
Like the **Family** Trauma
You can not escape from
You feel the pinch
You pull it out
Creating a larger wound
The type of wound
You cannot live without
Like a cactus it pricks

Morph

The mirror image shines back at you
The glare of the morning sun ☀
Causes your right eye to squint
Do you like what you see?
How does it make you feel?
Are you scared?
Are you curious?
What if you could simply morph
Into exactly what your brain wants?
What if you could be who you were always supposed to
be?
What if it were as simple as that?
Do your pants feel ok?
What about that dress?
What about the attention you get for the gender
You know longer feel aligned to
What about all of these things?
What about the pain, and the fear?
How does one measure these feelings?
Remember the first time you put on that bowtie?
It was the first time I smiled in ages
Ask yourself

The Seed

The sun reflects on the bright green leaf
It adds some rainbow to the room
It helps you to deal with your grief
Like that first sip of some ice cold juice
It was the moment you first felt something
It was that second you realized
That she was your muse
For the seed you have planted
Will grow like a weed
Is that person in your life
Exactly what you need?

The Controller

I always felt scared
Timid in fact
I was afraid of the questions
Didn't know how to act

It would be a long while
Before I'd be free
It took a long time
To actually feel **me**

There was pain, there were struggles
The damage was deep
An ache in my heart
I could no longer keep

Each fracture and feud
Sharpened as I got older
Each hug and hello
Felt a little bit colder
The controller

The Box ⌐┘

When I was a kid
I loved boxes so much
A place to hide things,
They were always enough
I would write little notes
And letters to myself
I would open it slowly
Like there was a monster inside
I pretended there were stars and rainbows in there
I imagined the fairy dust would make me fly
I was always a dreamer
Nothing felt impossible
Everything was real
When I was a kid

<u>Their</u>

My body
Your body
His Body
Her body
THEIR body
What serves you?
What hurts you?
What FEELS good to you?
What penetrates your body and soul?
What makes your heart beat, and your body tick?

Born with a love of the arts, Ellis James can often be found creating. They enjoy sculpting, watercolors, and writing. Ellis has many dear friends and family who have been the cornerstone of their progress towards self love and happiness.

Ellis loves making memories with their wife and two children. They live outside NYC with a grumpy old cat named Dante, AKA baby Dan.

✫ Follow Me ✫

Instagram:@ellisjamespoetry
Facebook:@ellisjamespoetry
TikTok:@ellisjamespoetry